CU00960966

One
Extremely Useful
Book of
Christmas

Lists

Copper Beech Publishing

The object of this Extremely Useful Book is to provide you with the perfect way to organise a successful festive celebration.

Overseas Cards

	SENT	REC'D

*Overseas
Gifts*

Cards Family

	SENT	REC'D
Uncle Charlie	✓	✓

Cards
Family

	SENT	REC'D

Cards
Family

	SENT	REC'D

In 1963 children writing to Father Christmas received a reply courtesy of the Post Office, and children still receive this service today.

December, 1963

FROM REINDEERLAND, N1

Dear Children,

Thanks to my good friends in the Post Office the nice letters you posted to me in Snowland, Toyland, etc., have been reaching me safely, and I am very pleased because I in turn can now write to each of you - but only if you have put your own full address on your letter.

The Post Office and I are extremely busy at this time of the year, delivering all your toys and everybody's presents, and because able to answer any letters that are posted af

Cards
Friends and Neighbours

	SENT	REC'D

Cards
Friends and Neighbours

	SENT	REC'D

London's first pillar box at the corner of Fleet Street and Farringdon Street, 1855.

Cards
Friends and Neighbours

	SENT	REC'D

Cards
Business

	SENT	REC'D

CHRISTMAS PRESENTS FOR ALL.

Some Seasonable Suggestions.

GRANDFATHER.
Reading Glass.
Book Holder.
Silk Muffler.
Reading Lamp.

GRANDMOTHER.
Spectacle Chatelaine
Dorothy Bag.   [Case.
Dainty Perfume.
Felt Slippers.

FATHER.
Pocket Stamp Case.
Flat Pocket Pencil.
Walking Stick.
Shaving Materials.
Smoking Coat.

MOTHER.
Card Case.
Initial Handkerchiefs.
Umbrella.
Favourite Poets.
Opera Glasses.

SONS.
Shoe-Blacking Case.
Tie Pin.
Watch Chain Charm.
Hanging Clothes Brushes.
Fancy Waistcoat.
Ring.

DAUGHTERS.
Glove and Handkerchief
Stock Ties.   [Case.
Fancy Hair-Combs.
Initial Brush and Comb.
Silk Blouse Length.
Bracelet.

FOR THE CHILDREN.
Money-box.
Waterproof Satchel.
Coloured Crayons.
Clockwork Train.
Music Case.
Muff and Fur.
Handkerchiefs.
Drawing Slate.

Books of Adventure.
Indoor Games.
Toy Soldiers.
Steam Engine.
Tea Set.
Fur-lined Gloves.
Box of Paints.
Dancing Slippers.

FOR THE BABY.
Silver Rattle.
Rag Doll.
Little Woollen Jacket.

Silver " Baby " Brooch.
Sleeve Tie-ups and Sash.
Silk Embroidered Bib.

FOR THE MAID.
Warm Gloves.
Caps.
Handkerchiefs.

Aprons.
House Shoes.
Warm Blouse.

These 'seasonable suggestions' were offered in
1904 in a woman's magaine.

🌿 *Gifts* *Family*		
Aunt Mary	*pink slippers*	✓

Gifts
Family

Gifts
Family

🎄 Gifts
Friends and Neighbours

Gifts
Friends and Neighbours

🌿 Special Gifts

Gifts
Business

The
Christmas Stocking

The tradition of the
Christmas Stocking
is said to have begun when
St Nicholas, wishing to
provide dowries for three poor
girls anonymously, threw
bags of gold through their
window which fell either into
their shoes on the hearth or
their stockings hanging by
the fire to dry.

The traditional contents
of the stocking are
not expensive, but symbolic
and should include
an apple for health;
an orange for a treat;
coal for warmth;
salt for good luck and a
new penny for wealth in the
year to come.

Gifts
Stocking Fillers

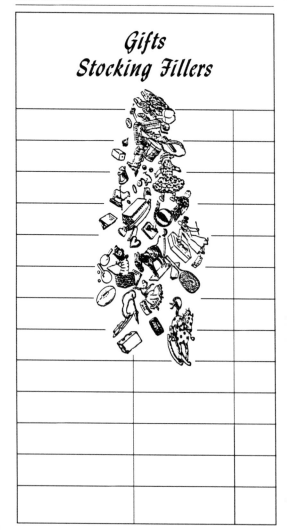

May Your
Christmas be
a Happy One
And may the
New Year bring
You Contentment
and Prosperity
in overflowing
measure.

Festive Fayre
Christmas Eve

Daytime Snacks

....
....
....
....
....
....
....

Supper

....
....
....
....
....
....
....

Festive Fayre
Christmas Eve

Order in advance

....
....
....
....
....
....
....

Last minute buys

....
....
....
....
....
....
....

Children can be kept busy by making place cards for tomorrow's Christmas table.

During the 19th century
many people had goose for
Christmas dinner and saved
up for it all year by paying
into a 'Goose Club'.

Victorian families took their
Christmas goose to the
local baker to be cooked
in his large oven
on Christmas morning.

Fruit and Nut 'Un-stuffing'

Ingredients required:-
Onions, celery, dried apricots, chestnuts (or walnuts), breadcrumbs, chopped fresh parsley, chopped fresh thyme, egg, salt, black pepper and a little butter.

The finely chopped onion should be sauteed with the chopped celery in the melted butter.
Add all other ingredients except egg and mix well.
Leave to cool then bind all ingredients with the egg.
Press into a well buttered dish and cook separately from the meat.
Serve with cranberry sauce.

Experiment with this before Christmas to combine just the right combination of fruit and nuts to your taste.

This fine creation will please those who do not eat meat, but who long for some of the rich flavours of Christmas.

Festive Fayre
Christmas Day

Breakfast

....
....
....
....
....

Christmas Dinner

....
....
....
....
....

Supper

....
....
....
....
....

Festive Fayre
Christmas Day

Order in advance

....
....
....
....
....
....

Last minute buys

....
....
....
....
....
....
....

Remember to plan time for telephone calls.

Plum pudding or pottage was originally a thick soup based on meat stock, bread, dried fruit and spices eaten at the start of the Christmas feast.

The silver charms sometimes added into the modern 'pudding' symbolise a coin for wealth, a ring for marriage and a thimble for a life of blessedness.

Traditional Christmas Pudding
(Serves 8, fits a 2 pint basin)

2 oz flour
1 level teaspoon mixed spice
1½ level teaspoon cinnamon
½ level teaspoon nutmeg
4oz mixed candied peel
4oz chopped blanched almonds
1 tablespoon black treacle
4oz fine breadcrumbs
4oz melted butter
4oz brown sugar
4oz grated apple
1 small carrot, grated
1lb mixed dried fruit, preferably:
8oz raisins, 4oz sultanas, 4oz currants
Grated rind and juice of 1 large lemon
2 eggs
¼ pint ale + 2 tablespoons brandy

Mix all ingredients thoroughly. Stir well and leave the mixture for 24 hours to mature. Press into large basin and cover with greased paper. Cover with paste made from 6oz flour and water to give firm dough; this keeps the pudding very dry. Steam or boil 6-8 hours. Remove damp covers and when cold put on dry paper. Steam a further 2-4 hours before serving.

Festive Fayre
Boxing Day

Breakfast

. . . .

. . . .

. . . .

. . . .

. . . .

Lunch

. . . .

. . . .

. . . .

. . . .

Supper

. . . .

. . . .

. . . .

. . . .

. . . .

Festive Fayre
Boxing Day

Order in advance

....
....
....
....
....
....

Last minute buys

....
....
....
....
....
....
....

Don't forget spare batteries for toys and bulbs
for the tree lights!

Beverages

Wine

....
....
....
....
....

Ales

....
....
....
....

Champagne

....
....
....
....
....

Beverages

Liqueurs & Spirits

....
....
....
....
....
....

Non-alcoholic

....
....
....
....

Fruit Juices & Mixers

....
....
....
....
....

TIME'S CHANGES.

On Christmas Eve, long, long ago,
  I heard small Kitty lisping low,
"Tum an' tiss me, Tousin Joe,
  Underneaf de mistletoe!"
And he replied impatiently,
  "Run away, you bother me!
Naughty Kitty, don't you see
  I'm as busy as can be?"

But that was many years ago.
  To-night, beneath the mistletoe,
I hear his voice, entreating, low—
  "Kiss me, sweetheart; kiss poor Joe!"
And Kitty says coquettishly,
  "Go away, you bother me!
Naughty Joseph, don't you see
  I'm as busy as can be?"

Old-Fashioned Mulled Wine

1 bottle rich red wine
1 pint water
3oz sugar
1 lemon and one orange,
both stuck with cloves and roasted by the fire
1 tablespoon fruit liqueur
1 teaspoon ground ginger
1 stick cinnamon

Bring all ingredients to a gentle simmer. Add additional slices of fruit and leave to brew on the fire for some time. Ladle into glasses.

Decoration

Living Room

Dining Room

Hall

Decoration

Children's Rooms

....

....

....

....

....

....

Front Door and Outside

....

....

....

....

....

....

....

....

 Mistletoe

*Years ago, mistletoe was thought to have
powers of fertility - which is possibly why
we kiss under it
You have been warned!*

❄ *Tree Decorations* ❄
*The earliest Christmas tree decorations
were candles, gilded fruit and nuts, sweets
and small gifts.*

🔔 The Tree

Baubles	✓

❄ *The Christmas Tree* ❄

Prince Albert popularised the tree in this country by making it the centre of the Royal Family Christmas.

The Table

Crackers .... ✓

 Mince Pies

Oliver Cromwell banned the eating of mince pies which were only reintroduced in 1660 at the Restoration.

The Table

'Here we come a-wassailing...'
*Wassail comes from the Anglo-Saxon 'Wes hal'
meaning 'be whole' - the equivalent of drinking to
'your very good health'.*

The Christmas Cracker

*The Christmas Cracker
based on the French Bon Bon,
came to England from France in
the mid 19th century.*

*It is usually accepted that the
confectioner Tom Smith
introduced the idea and created
the modern form by adding
first the motto then the snap
and finally the novelty and
paper hat.*

"MOTOR CYCLE" CRACKERS
1913/14 No 937 Per
dozen boxes 15/-

Involving the children...

Orange Pomanders

Years ago, the aroma from these pomanders would disguise unpleasant smells.

Push cloves (stalk end first) into the orange. Tie ribbon around the orange and hang on the Christmas tree.

Candle Lamps

Using a clean jar and enamel paint, draw Father Christmas, a snowman or a tree, dot on the snow effect with white paint and put a night light candle in the bottom of the jar.

Glittering Holly

Paint glue around the edge of each leaf, then gently add glitter (using newspaper to catch the excess, which can be used again).

Miniature Trees

Let the children have a miniature tree in their rooms and decorate it themselves!

Festive Diary

Children's Parties

Lunch Parties

Drinks Parties

Dinner

Entertaining

Dinner-Dance

Guests to Stay

Festive Diary

Christmas Eve

Christmas Day

Boxing Day

Guests to Stay

Guests..
Arriving...
Departing...

Beds		Special Notes
Spare Covers		
Towels		
Flowers		
Books		

Guests..
Arriving...
Departing...

Beds		Special Notes
Spare Covers		
Towels		
Flowers		
Books		

Guests to Stay

Guests..

Arriving..

Departing..

Beds		*Special Notes*
Spare Covers		
Towels		
Flowers		
Books		

Guests..

Arriving..

Departing..

Beds		*Special Notes*
Spare Covers		
Towels		
Flowers		
Books		

Party Games

Baby Photographs

All visitors are asked to bring along a photograph taken when they were a child - and preferably at Christmas time. These photographs are marked or numbered in some way and arranged about the room. All visitors are then given pencils and papers already numbered, and asked to guess whose photographs they are.

Earth Air and Water

One of the players, who sit round in a circle, throws a balloon to another, at the same time calling "Earth" (or "Air," or "Water," as he likes), and counting aloud up to 'ten.' The one to whom he has directed the balloon must give the name of some animal that lives on the earth (or, if "air" be called, of some bird; if "water," of some fish) before the thrower has counted ten, paying a forfeit if he fails. That player sends the balloon on to some one else and so on. No animal bird or fish may be repeated. Those not able to think of a creature sit out until there is a winner remaining.

*If you have enjoyed using this
book of Christmas Lists we would like
to hear from you. Is there anything
you would like to find next year? Did
you have enough pages for card lists /
gift lists / menu planning? Of course we
can't guarantee to put everyone's
suggestion into next year's book, but
this is your book, and it should assist
you in your festive planning.
We would welcome your comments!*

First published in Great Britain in 1994 by
Copper Beech Publishing Ltd

ISBN 1-898617-01-5

Additional research by Maureen Brant.

Copper Beech Gift Books
are printed and bound in Great Britain.

Shopping List

....
....
....
....
....
....
....
....
....
....
....
....
....
....
....
....
....
....
....

Party Games

Family Coach

This game has been played by school-aged children for over 100 years. The players must sit round the room and each choose some part of the family coach - the wheel, the axle, the whip, the seat, Mrs Brown, her baby, the cat, etc., etc.

One of the grown-ups must then tell the tale of Mrs Brown's journey in the coach, and of the accidents that befell them; how one of the wheels came off, the axle broke, the baby cried, and so on, making it up as she goes along. At the mention of each specific part, the member who has chosen that part must stand up and turn round. But should the words "Family Coach" be mentioned, all the players must change their seats. Should any fail to do this, or to answer his cue when his part is mentioned, he must pay a forfeit.

Extra paper and pencils plus some wrapped novelties for prizes will be invaluable.

Thank You!

We're leaving these pages for you to make notes of gifts received and thank you letters to be written after Christmas is over.

....

....

....

....

....

....

....

....

....

....

....

....

....

....

....

....

Thank You!

....

....

....

....

....

....

....

....

....

....

....

....

....

....

....

....

....

Evergreens have been brought into the house at midwinter since Roman times. They bring good luck and symbolise eternal life.

Holly and Ivy represent Man and Woman and their struggle for mastery in the house. If prickly holly is brought in first the man will have mastery. Smooth holly first gives the wife the upper hand.

Shopping List

Victorian postmen wore red uniforms and were called Robin Postmen.

Shopping List

*Boxing Day
was when the Almsboxes
were opened in churches for
the poor and tradesmen
broke into the earthenware
boxes which held the
annual tips from their
customers.*